Spot the Difference

Mouths

Daniel Nunn

Heinemann Library
Chicago, Illinois

© 2007 Heinemann Library
a division of Reed Elsevier Inc.
Chicago, Illinois

Customer Service   888–454–2279

Visit our website at www.heinemannlibrary.com

Photo research by Erica Newbery
Designed by Jo Hinton-Malivoire
Printed and bound in China by South China Printing Company
10 09 08 07 06
10 9 8 7 6 5 4 3 2 1

Library of Congress Cataloging-in-Publication Data
Nunn, Daniel.
  Mouths / Daniel Nunn.
      p. cm. — (Spot the difference)
  Includes bibliographical references and index.
  ISBN 1-4034-8475-9 (hc) — ISBN 1-4034-8480-5 (pb)
  1. Mouth—Juvenile literature. I. Title. II. Series.
  QL857.N86 2007
  591.4'4—dc22
                          2006007241

Acknowledgments
The author and publisher are grateful to the following for permission to reproduce copyright material:
Alamy p. **6** (Alaska Stock LLC); Corbis pp. **5** (Gary W Carter), **9** (Tom Brakefield), **12** (Amos Nachoum), **14** (Joe McDonald), **15** (Steve Kaufman), **18** (Zefa/Bach); FLPA p. **17** (Minden Pictures/Mitsuaki Iwago); Getty Images pp. **13** (Lonely Planet Image/David Tipling), **16** (Photodisc Green/John Giustina), **19** (Photodisc Green/Dick Luria), **21** (The Image Bank/Peter Dazeley); Harcourt Education/Tudor Photography p. **7**; Nature Picture Library pp. **4** (Pete Oxford), **8** (Anup Shah), **10** (Jane Burton), **11** (Tony Heald), **20** (Vincent Munier).

Cover image of a hippopotamus's mouth reproduced with permission of Steve Bloom.

Every effort has been made to contact copyright holders of any material reproduced in this book. Any omissions will be rectified in subsequent printings if notice is given to the publisher.

Contents

What Is a Mouth?

mouth

Many animals have a mouth.

Animals use their mouth to eat.

Animals use their mouth to breathe air.

Animals have their mouth on their head.

Different Shapes and Sizes

Mouths come in many shapes.
Mouths come in many sizes.

This is a tiger.
It has a big mouth.

mouth

This is a sea horse.
It has a small mouth.

This is a crocodile.
It has a long mouth.

This is a shark.
It has a wide mouth.

This is a woodpecker.
It has a sharp mouth.

Amazing Mouths

This is a pelican.
It uses its mouth to scoop up fish.

This is a lion.
It uses its mouth to carry its cub.

This is a dog.
It uses its mouth to play.

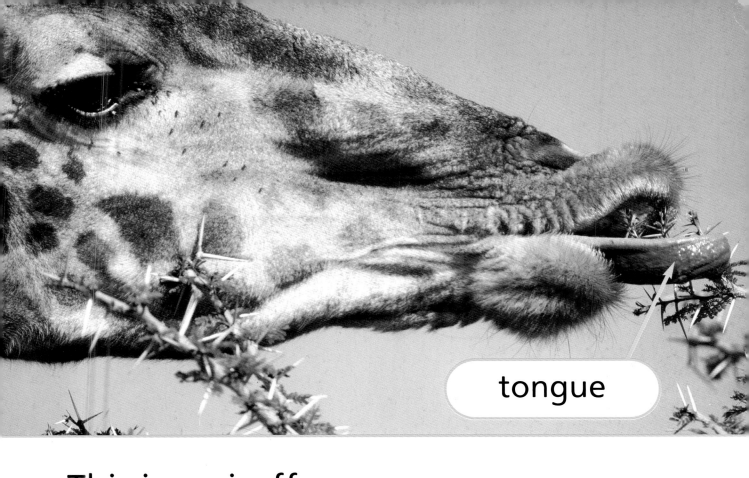

tongue

This is a giraffe.
It uses its mouth to pull leaves
off trees.

17

tongue

This is a frog.
It uses its mouth to catch food.

teeth

This is a beaver.
It uses its mouth to cut down trees.

Mouths and You

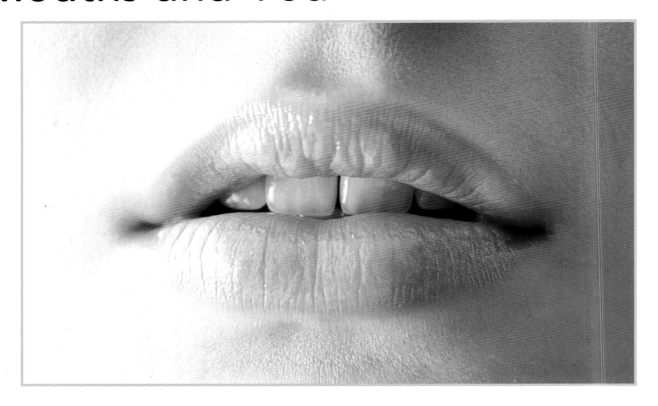

People have a mouth, too.

People use their mouth to eat.
People use their mouth to breathe air.
People are like other animals.

Spot the Difference!

How many differences can you see?

Picture Glossary

breathe take in air

scoop lift something up like you are using a spoon

sharp able to cut into something

Index

Note to Parents and Teachers

National science standards recommend that young children understand that animals have different parts that serve distinct functions. In *Mouths*, children are introduced to mouths and how they are used to eat and breathe. The text and photographs allow children to recognize and compare how mouths can be alike and different across a diverse group of animals, including humans.

The text has been carefully chosen with the advice of a literacy expert to enable beginning readers' success while reading independently or with moderate support. An animal expert was consulted to provide both interesting and accurate content.

You can support children's nonfiction literacy skills by helping them to use the table of contents, headings, picture glossary, and index.